Phonetic Bible Stories

Jesus Feeds the 5,000

John 6:9–13

Little
Is Big

Claudia Courtney ☆ **Illustrated by Reg Sandland**

For my children, Kellie and Matthew,
who know God uses even the little ones.

Copyright © 1998 Concordia Publishing House
3558 S. Jefferson Avenue, St. Louis, MO 63118-3968
Manufactured in the United States of America

1 2 3 4 5 6 7 8 9 10   07 06 05 04 03 02 01 00 99 98

Note to Grown-ups

The love of reading is one of the greatest things you can instill in your child. It opens new horizons, exposes your child to new ideas, and provides information as well as entertainment.

This beginning reader series blends the best of two worlds—phonics to help your child learn to read and popular Bible stories to help your child learn to read God's Word. After you use a book in this series, open your child's Bible and read the story from God's Word. Emphasize to your child that this story is not make-believe—it's true, and we can believe every word in God's Holy Book.

Before you begin, review together the word, sound, and spelling lists on page 16. This story emphasizes the short *i* sound, as in the words *little* and *big*. The numerals 5 and 2 are used instead of the words because *five* has the long $\bar{i}$ sound and is not in keeping with the phonetic focus of the story.

After your review, read the story to your child, exaggerating the designated phonetic sound or sounds. Discuss the illustrations. Your enthusiasm for reading, and especially for reading God's Word, should be contagious. Run your finger under each word as you read it, showing your child that it is the words that convey the actual story. Have your child join with you in reading repeated phrases.

Finally, have your child read the story as you offer plenty of praise. Pause to allow your youngster time to sound out words, but provide help when necessary to avoid frustration. When a mistake is made, invite your child to reread the sentence. This provides an appropriate opportunity to guide your early reader.

Please remember that your child is learning and blending a complex set of new skills. Early success and your generous praise are keys to opening the door to your child's world of reading, especially to the joys of reading the Bible.

Claudia Courtney

The people are hungry.
What will they eat?

5 little loaves.
2 little fish.

A little boy will share his dinner.
He will give it to Jesus.

5 little loaves.
2 little fish.

The dinner is too little.
The crowd is too big.

Jesus takes the dinner.
He gives thanks to God.

His friends give the food to
the crowd.

5 little loaves.
2 little fish.
Nibble, nibble, nibble.
Still there is more.

The boy does not miss his dinner.
He eats his fill.
So do all the people.
They do not wish for another dish.

5 little loaves.
2 little fish.
Nibble, nibble, nibble.
Still there is more.

Friends fill 12 baskets with
tidbits of food.
A little is big with Jesus.

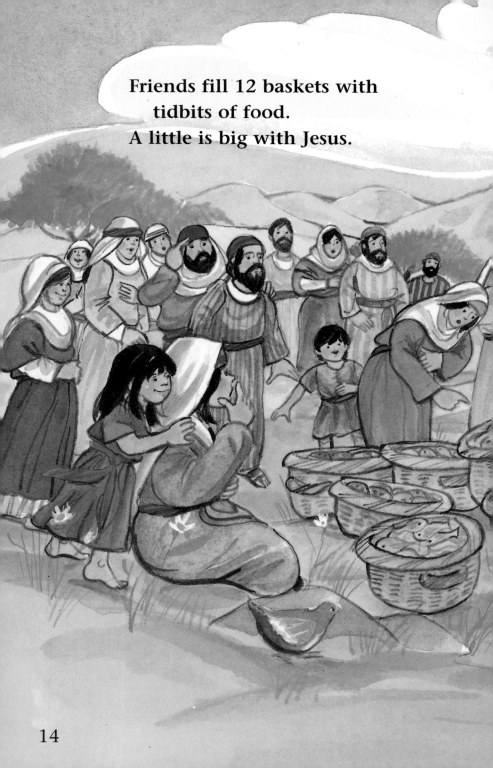

The people give thanks.
Hip! Hip! Hooray!
A little is big with Jesus.

Word Lists

short *i* words	Other Words	
big	2	loaves
dinner	5	more
dish	12	not
fill	a	of
fish	all	people
give	another	share
gives	are	so
hip	baskets	takes
his	boy	thanks
is	crowd	the
it	do	there
little	does	they
miss	eat	to
nibble	eats	too
still	food	what
tidbits	for	
will	friends	
wish	God	
with	he	
	hooray	
	hungry	
	Jesus	